D1518775

May all your mice be dead!

Dedicated to the Children
of
Medical Examiners, Coroners, Forensic
Pathologists, Forensic Anthropologists,
Forensic Odontologists, Death Scene
Investigators, Anatomists, Funeral
Directors, Crematorium Operators,
Embalmers, Taxidermists,
Very Good Hunters,
and Really Bad Veterinarians.

Once upon a time, and early one morning,
Ted and Sally were playing by a creek
when they discovered a dead mouse that
had drowned in a puddle of water.
They picked the mouse up and spent the
rest of the day playing with it.

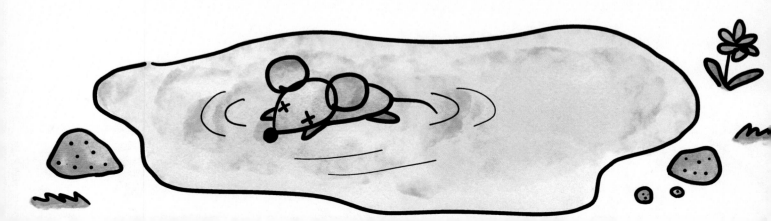

They named the mouse Maggie and took her to the kitchen to show Grandma Molly, but Grandma Molly wouldn't let them bring Maggie inside.

Maggie was so much fun.
Ted and Sally took her
everywhere.
She seemed content riding
in Ted's shirt pocket.

Ted and Sally soon discoverd,
to their amazement, that Maggie
was not just any dead mouse...
Maggie was a magic mouse
that could play games and do
tricks!

Maggie was excellent at playing freeze tag. Sally would lean Maggie against a rock and Maggie would stand totally still, never moving a muscle, not even her tail.

Then Ted and Sally discovered that Maggie could do tricks. When she was laid down at the top of a hill and given a little nudge, Maggie would roll over... and over ... and over, all the way to the bottom of the hill. Their dog Max couldn't do that.

Maggie could also play dead. Sally would say, "play dead Maggie" and Maggie would lay perfectly still. When Max played dead, his tail would wag, but Maggie's tail never wiggled even one bit.

When placed in a bucket of water,
Ted and Sally discovered that
Maggie could actually swim,
well maybe not swim... but she
was great at floating!

The most amazing thing Maggie the Magic Dead Mouse could do was fly. Of course, Ted would have to assist a little. Ted would wind up his throwing arm and let Maggie go high in the air.

Maggie, with Ted's help, could easily fly 15 feet, but Ted was certain she could fly a record 20 feet. So, Ted wound his arm up and threw with all his might. Maggie flew higher than ever.
But then...

A crow swooped down and caught Maggie
in its beak and flew away with her.

Ted and Sally waved goodbye and were amazed at how easy Maggie could make new friends. She had barely known the crow, but off they went together — already best of friends.
Maggie was indeed a Magic Dead Mouse.

The end.

Let's ask a professional

How would my death have been investigated in the real world — if I had been a person?

Hi, I'm Dr. Berryman. I'm a forensic anthoropologist. I can answer that question, Maggie. First, the kids should have immediately called the police to report finding you, of course if you were a person.

I know… I know, but since I'm a dead mouse, I'm treated differently. So, what would happen when the police were called?

Police and a death investigator from the medical examiner's or coroner's office would come to the scene of the puddle and investigate to see why the person was there. The people who found the dead person would have been questioned.

But wait Dr. Berryman, the children took me with them, and we spent the day playing. What would happen if someone took the dead person away before the police and death investigator arrived at the scene?

That would have been a very serious mistake. In real life, you should not touch or move anything. Anyone who touches anything would be committing a crime and possibly charged with obstruction of justice, destruction of evidence, abuse of a corpse, or even more serious offenses.

So, Ted and Sally could have been arrested and charged with a crime!

Ted and Sally wouldn't have been arrested Maggie, because you're a dead mouse, not a person.

Oh yea . . . since my death, I haven't thought nearly as clearly. But what would happen if a dead person had been moved?

Nothing could happen until the dead person was found again. Often by that time, only bones are left.

How would it ever be found again?

Sometime, a person may know what happened and tell police where to look, but many times the bones are found by accident. Perhaps a farmer, or a hiker, of anyone else might find the bones and call the police.

Okay . . . just for fun, let's say a hiker found my bones. How would my skeleton be investigated?

First, the hiker would call the police and the police would call the medical examiner's or coroner's office and tell them they need assistance with a scene that has skeletal remains.

Wow, that's exciting! What happens next?

The medical examiner or coroner would send one of their death investigators and ask their forensic anthropologist to go with them.

Now I'm confused, but I'm a dead mouse, so that's probably the reason. Why do you keep saying medical examiner OR coroner?

Some states have medical examiners who are appointed, and other states have coroners who are elected.

Oh, I suspect there is a lot more to this than you can tell a dead mouse in a children's book. But why can't the police handle this? Why do they call the medical examiner or coroner?

The police are responsible for handling and investigating the scene, while the medical examiner or coroner is responsible for the dead person, or mouse skeleton in this case.

So, the death investigator goes to the scene to represent the medical examiner or coroner, right?

Yes Maggie! Great answer . . . for a dead mouse!

What does the forensic anthropologist do that the death investigator can't do?

The death investigators' education and training gives them a deep biological knowledge that makes them ideal for investigating a person's death, while the forensic anthropologists' education and training deals with the skeleton of people and animals. There are 206 bones in a person's body and a forensic anthropologist must know every one of them.

So, what would you, the forensic anthropologist, do when you arrived at the scene with my skeleton?

With my training, I would immediately identify your bones as animal bones of no forensic significance. The police would release the scene, remove the yellow crime scene tape and we would all go home.

Wait a minute. My bones are so small that hikers would never have called the police. They would have known my bones were too small to be from a person.

Not necessarily, forensic anthropologists may receive bones from an infant or even a fetus.

Wow . . . forensic anthropologists sure are intelligent!

Yes . . . yes we are Maggie.

I was last seen with a crow. What might you find on my bones that could be important?

With a skeleton, I sometime find evidence of what happened to the person. I might find gunshot wounds, blunt trauma fractures and cut marks but I often find evidence of scavenger activity. All of this would be presented in a formal report to the medical examiner or corner.

If you looked at my bones, you would probably find bird beak marks. That crow was no friend!

If I found no evidence of gunshot wounds, blunt trauma or cut marks, the medical examiner or coroner would list both your cause of death and manner of death as undetermined. Ted and Sally found you floating in a puddle. For the first time, I get to ask a dead mouse what was your *actual* cause and manner of death?

I drowned, that was my cause of death, and my manner of death wasn't natural, homicide or suicide, it was accidental. I stole a piece of cheese from Grandma Molly's kitchen and accidentally dropped it in the puddle. I waded into the puddle and got over my head . . . I drowned.

Maggie, any last words of wisdom?

Yes . . . never go into water until you learn how to swim!

Made in the USA
Middletown, DE
11 December 2024

66672447R00015